Lateral Thinking

HOW TO APPLY LATERAL THINKING TO EVERYDAY LIFE

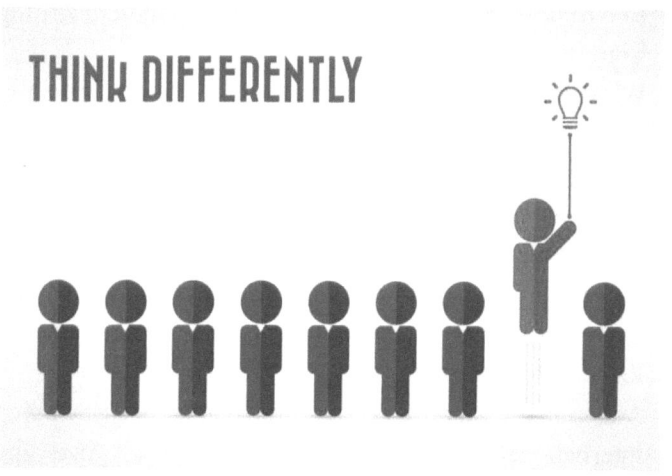

A GUIDE ON EXPANDING YOUR CREATIVE HORIZONS

CHRIS SMYTHE

Copyright © 2019 by Chris Smythe
All Rights Reserved

Disclaimer:

No part of this publication may be reproduced or transmitted in any form or by any means, or transmitted electronically without direct written permission in writing from the author.

While all attempts have been made to verify the information provided in this publication, neither the author nor the publisher assumes any responsibility for errors, omissions, or misuse of the subject matter contained in this eBook.

This eBook is for entertainment purposes only, and the views expressed are those of the author alone, and should not be taken as expert instruction. The reader is responsible for their own actions.

Adherence to applicable laws and regulations, including international, federal, state, and local governing professional licensing business practices, advertising, and all other aspects of doing business in the U.S.A, Canada or any other jurisdiction is the sole responsibility of the purchaser or reader.

Contents

Introduction v

Chapter 1: What is Lateral Thinking aka
            "Thinking outside of the box?" 1
   It is very easy to get tricked and manipulated
   by the smallest opinion of others. 3

Chapter 2: Why we do what we do. 7

Chapter 3: Social conditioning and the
            impact of our decisions. 12

Chapter 4: "Thinking outside of the box" 18

Chapter 5: Why we must think differently? 25

Chapter 6: Risk management, fear of
            making decisions and changes. 31

Thinking almost always brings somewhat
of a change. And people are afraid
of changes...32
Thinking can bring us doubt and
insecurity, as well as responsibility. 33
Talk to people more and open up to
others about your beliefs and opinions...............38
Be humble. It's not possible for you to
learn and see things differently when
you think you know everything already 39

**Chapter 7: Understanding that you cannot
always be right 41**
Having some self-confidence to admit
that you've made a mistake. 43
Being brave and courageous when it
comes to making a change. 43
Practicing by creating different scenarios
and situations with many possible
outcomes in your mind 44

**Chapter 8: Your emotion is your only
compass. Learn to always
listen to your heart. 45**
Live in harmony, fully understand,
accept and embrace who you are. 46
Listening to your heart 48

Conclusion... 51

Introduction

Living in a modern society is not easy. Maybe we sometimes look back at the people that lived way before us in the age where no technology existed and we tend to feel sorry for them because we think it was much harder living back then, but trust me, they had one thing that is much more valuable than technology or anything else that we have in the modern age. It is the peace of mind. And what does a peace of mind help us with? The most important thing that humans were created to do. Thinking correctly, freely and **without the influence of others**. Unlike people today, they didn't have any worry about what others thought about them and they certainly did not do things against their will just so they can feel like they fit in. They lived their lives freely and the way they wanted. The only way life is meant to be lived.

Before I begin, I want you to read and give a completely honest answer to all of my following questions.

Do you maybe sometimes feel like you're doing something against your will or making a certain decision without really being sure why exactly you're doing it? Do you often look at what others are doing and decide that you should be doing those exact same things, just so that you can be accepted in the community and feel like a part of it? Do you feel like a black sheep in the herd if you're the only one that's doing something differently from all your friends or family? Are you afraid of making changes? Do you often spend time on social media or in front of a TV screen watching reality shows or following celebrities? Is the fear of failure dragging you down and pushing you far away from reaching your goals and making your dreams come true?

If the answer is "YES" to any of these questions, then I really think you might want to reconsider the way you think, your decision-making abilities and honestly ask yourself if you are living the way you truly want or simply living to please the others around you.

In this book, I will personally share my own experiences, interesting situations and thoughts with you, and help you to clear your mind of all the anxiety, worry and constantly remind you that you don't have to care about being like the others around you or think a certain way just because others are.

It is time to start using your mind the way it should be used, make the decisions that are right and beneficial for you and remember who you really were before society or social media told you who you are.

I will give my best to make you realize some of the very important details, aspects and secrets of life that you might have missed while you were stuck in the endless loop of modern life and help you learn how to start thinking on your own and do what is best for you. I will be talking about the <u>Lateral Thinking</u> method also known as "Thinking outside of the Box", explaining how it works and why it is very beneficial for us to learn it and utilize it in our everyday life. I will also cover many different topics on how we think, why sometimes our decisions are very influenced by the others, how most of the people are forced to think a certain way since their young age, how to admit that you've made a mistake and utilize it as a lesson in life, why changes are a very necessary thing in life, how other people easily get tricked into changing their beliefs and much more.

I am going to teach you all of the useful elements which I applied when I was learning how to **"Think outside of the Box".** I will talk to you about the traditional "vertical thinking" method and its flaws and ultimately transfer all of my valuable knowledge and experience to you. Remember, if you don't want to change yourself, nobody else can. Change starts from within, and if you learn the importance of it, learn how to utilize Lateral Thinking and overall understand the way our brain works, you will be able to master the way you think and live a much happier and fulfilling life.

Without further ado, let's dive deep into our first chapter. It will be a long and wonderful journey full of interesting stories and experiences that happened in my past, as well as many situations that require good decision-making abilities in which you might find yourself in at any moment of your life.

CHAPTER 1:

What is Lateral Thinking aka "Thinking outside of the box?"

The purpose of why we think is to be able to collect information and attempt to make the best possible use out of it. Because of how our mind works and creates patterns, we are not able to make the best use out of the new information unless we find a way to reconstruct the old patterns and bring them up to date. Not everyone can do this because from our very young age we are trained to use the traditional thinking method. The "traditional" method that we use or also known as "vertical thinking" only teaches us how to select some of the already existing patterns and make a decision through a process of elimination. However, we will never get the best out of our decisions if we don't learn how to utilize the Lateral Thinking method.

Lateral thinking or "Thinking outside of the box" is a term used to describe a method of solving problems or making decisions by using a more indirect or "unusual" and creative approach, most often by looking at the "problem" from a different perspective. People who are such thinkers are not worried about the opinions of others and always tend to make decisions that are good for them, regardless if someone else thinks otherwise. Lateral thinking is very tightly related to creativity, humor, and insight. By utilizing all of these things our mind is able to re-wire and make a superior decision and get the best out of every situation that we find ourselves in.

Here are a few examples to help you understand better. Many people often start to do what their family or friends do, just so that they can feel like a part of the group. For example, I personally know many people who really and I mean really dislike smoking cigarettes but they started doing it because everyone else in their friend circle was smoking, or because the girl that they liked smoked as well and they just wanted to fit in or impressed them. They are going against their will and in this case against their health just so they feel more comfortable. Another example is when a friend calls you and says that he watched a movie and that movie was awful, so If you watch it, you will constantly see everything in a bad light and nothing will impress you. This is because your friend's opinion matters a lot to you and can often blur out your real perception of things. The same would be if you were to buy a pair of jeans and your friend tells you that they look very good on your body even though they don't. You will still convince yourself that they do match you, just because he said so.

It is very easy to get tricked and manipulated by the smallest opinion of others.

Here is a short story from when I was in high school.

I went out to a party with a friend from my class. Before going there, we both agreed that we will just stay sober, socialize with others and have a good "chill" time without drinking much or do anything crazy. At some point in the night, a group of guys from our class came and we clearly saw that they are under the effect of psychedelic drugs. I suggested to my friend that we leave and go somewhere else to avoid a problem. Sadly, we were not really quick in our decision making and they got real close to us. We got into a small talk and they started making fun of my friend because he wasn't drinking or doing any drugs, and knowing his personality, he got really upset and worried that they will keep teasing him about it if he doesn't prove them wrong. His ego was very fragile and without much hesitation, he asked them to give him whatever they took and he will prove to them that he is not what they think he is. After a few attempts to stop him, I finally gave up because all he cared about is the reputation "he would get" if he just stopped being a coward. I made a final attempt at convincing him that this is a very bad decision, but he just swallowed the pills. After half an hour, he is laying on a hospital bed, his father is talking to the police, his mom can't stop crying and my parents are freaking out and yelling at me saying that I was supposed to be the one to stop him from doing that. After a two week period when everything settles down, he comes back to school and guesses what happens. Not only that they didn't stop calling him a coward, but they also made fun of him even more now for being "weak" and getting sick from just a couple of pills.

LATERAL THINKING

The point of my story is that by making one bad decision just so that he can be what someone else wants him to be, he created even more problems for himself. He worsened his health and now he is being teased and called out even more. Not to mention all of the punishments from his parents and the bad picture that he left in everyone's eyes.

If he would just reject doing drugs, everyone would look at him like a smart guy who can stand up for himself and make smart decisions. Maybe he would even convince those guys who teased him that drugs are bad for their health. He is a smart guy, but his worry about being accepted in a certain group and the need to prove himself all the time to someone is what really ruined him. In this example my friend was thinking using the traditional "vertical thinking" method, he excluded one out of two situations and picked the one he thought will be the best which later reflected really bad on him. Instead, if he used the lateral thinking method he would be able to create new pathways and create a situation that is to his advantage. He could've politely reject doing drugs, start a talk about how drugs are bad and unhealthy and how they should stop using them as well. This would make the group of guys look at him in a completely different light and instead of calling him a coward they will form an image in their heads that he is, in fact, a smart guy and he worries about their good being. He could've been the hero of the night instead of ending up in the hospital bed, and he could've made some new friends as well. This way he ended up getting the worst-case scenario because in his mind there were only two options, he did not see the countless other ones because he was thinking vertically.

My example might have been a little harsh, but it's the sad truth and this happens almost all the time in our everyday lives. We need to constantly ask ourselves why we're doing something and is it the right thing to do. Let "is this truly what I want" be the phrase you always hear in your mind before doing something. Taking drugs was not what he wanted at all, he wanted to be appreciated and accepted and he thought that there is only one way to do it.

CHAPTER 2:

Why we do what we do.

In the introduction part, I mentioned a term called "following the herd".

This is often used to describe someone who blindly follows a group (or so-called a "herd") without questioning their decisions or thinking for themselves. Sometimes the "sheep" is a person who was just raised and "taught" to follow what others are doing without questioning in order to avoid risks or other sorts of challenges. Even if it may sound a bit weird at first, people like this really exist. They just want to be in their comfort zones so much that it doesn't even matter to them that they're completely the same as somebody else. They don't know the powers, qualities and unique capabilities that they possess, and usually, when someone tries to talk to them about it, they would get angry. Others are heavily influenced by social media and they tend to look at celebrities or some of the idols that they have and try to live, look or act exactly like them.

They try to wear the same types of clothes, dye their hair the same color, try to talk with their accent, get the same tattoos and maybe even change their religion like them. They change their image completely just so they can look or feel like them.

I will begin this chapter with another example, also a real story that happened to me in my teen years as well.

I was out with a group of friends in a park just having a good time and listening to some music. Suddenly a discussion about religion pops out and everyone engages in it. After some time a guy that sits right next to me is asked the next question: Are you religious and do you believe in God?

His answer was the following:

I am very religious, I go to church every week and I pray on the table with my family before eating dinner, but I do not believe in God.

Everyone just stopped talking for a minute and gave him a very confused look. A girl then asks him: Why would you do all of those things if you simply don't believe in God?

He says:

I do all of those things because everyone in my family is doing it. They are very religious and if they find out that I'm not, they will never look at me the same way and probably see me as a heretic and I will feel like an outcast. I'm afraid to tell them that I just don't believe, so I just keep pretending that I do and keep getting involved in their religious activities.

This is the moment when I realized that some people are just doing things because they're afraid to be different and honest with themselves. I understand that in the dark ages being a non-believer was a problem, I really do, but I honestly think that in modern times people should not feel like black sheep just because they don't want to follow a certain religion or some kind of a movement.

The sad truth is that people tend to do what others do, they like a certain type of music just because their friends like the same, not realizing that the ones who stand out and are unique, are usually the most attractive and smart people in everyone's eyes.

If you don't like a certain song, tell your friends why. Give out your opinion on it. If someone asks you if their shirt looks good on them when it really doesn't, give them the harsh truth. Don't say things that are not true and against your will hoping that someone will like you more because of it. You're just doing them a favor by telling them the truth. You will actually be surprised by how many people will appreciate your honest thoughts and most likely thank you for them. In a society where everyone lies to impress others, be a beacon of honesty and pure thoughts, it's the most attractive thing ever. And if someone gets mad at and starts insulting you for telling the truth, it means you only did yourself a favor, they just let you know that they were never a good person and you don't need those kinds of people in your life.

People need to get out of their comfort zones, they need to have their own strong opinions about the things that they like or dislike. They need to stand up and fight for what they love even if it means losing a "friend" or leaving a bad impression on someone. Stop looking and taking examples from famous people on social media or reality shows. If they buy expensive

LATERAL THINKING

cars, clothes and god knows what else, it does not mean that you have to be exactly like them. We are constantly being manipulated and have fake images created in our minds about how we are supposed to look, dress, eat or talk. Stop worrying about not having enough money to buy expensive clothes whatever reason you need them for, beauty comes from within.

Stop worrying and stressing about what others think, it's your own life and you need to live it the way you want, not the way others want.

CHAPTER 3:

Social conditioning and the impact of our decisions.

Social conditioning is a term used to describe a process when individuals are being trained in a society to have certain beliefs, emotional reactions, desires and wishes, behaviors and things of that nature, which are approved by that same society in general or by some groups that are part of it.

This social conditioning process usually begins from your very early age and it is most effective or "acute" during your childhood and adolescence, but it can keep going through your entire life. This is almost always carried by teachers, people in your community, parents, the TV shows that you watch, the novels that you read, the church that you go to every Sunday, the ads that you see and media as a whole and many other factors.

It does not really matter if you are aware of it or not, but we are being conditioned to act and do things in a certain way just because others around us are doing it.

The sad thing is that social conditioning usually works in a way by repeating and putting things in our brains millions and millions of times until our consciousness finally gives up and absorbs all of the unhealthy information. For example, every time you turn on a TV you see a guy that is dressed in expensive brands and has big muscles and the girls "drool" over him, which slowly puts an image in your mind that if you dress expensively or if you get big muscles girls will automatically "drool" over you as well.

Ever since we were kids our parents taught us to socialize with others and do activities together. Even if this sounds like a good thing, in some cases it can really be bad when it comes to our decision making. We learn to constantly look at others and what they're doing and if we do something different we start feeling guilty and worry that we're not "normal". Ask yourself an honest question. What does really "being normal" mean to you? What does even "normal" mean to you as a term? I'll give you ten seconds to answer.

Is your answer similar to this?

"Being normal means doing what everyone else is doing. "

If it is, then we have a problem.

It's time for a life story again..

There is a 16-year-old boy called James that really enjoys playing video games. He spends most of his time after school playing online. His parents realize that simply their kid loves what he's doing and doesn't force him to stop doing it. He has some friends from school, not all of them like playing video games, but he has one that really does. That friend's name is Rick. They both play games together and are very passionate about it, but unlike James's parents, Rick's parents constantly yell at him for doing it. They think video games are going to ruin him and that playing them is not "normal" at all. Instead, he must do things that are "normal". Rick is being forced to go outside when he doesn't want and forced to play football which he really hates. This impacts Rick's emotions because he's torn away from doing what he loves, this translates to him losing attention in class because he constantly thinks about video games, then he starts getting bad grades and gets punished at home. His parents still think that they're doing a good job. Meanwhile, James is happy because his parents let him do what he loves, he has really good grades and he is slowly becoming very good at the game he plays. A few years go by and now James is a professional gamer with a good salary, he is given a scholarship to many different high-grade universities and becomes pretty famous among others. He starts meeting new friends because of it and he is living his dream. Rick on the opposite is now left with nothing. He is not good at football because he hates doing it, he doesn't have a scholarship because his grades are bad and he's very sad because his parents restricted him from making his dreams come true. This is a prime example of how forcing someone to do something that is considered "normal" can only have a very bad impact on the person.

The point of this story is that people sometimes are forced since their young age to do something they hate just because someone else thinks it is right and "normal".

Nobody should be forced to be "normal" and do what others do. Everyone should get a chance to make their dreams come true. If you are brave, believe in your goals and constantly get out of your comfort zone, you will always reach your goals.

You should not upgrade your phone every year because everyone else is doing it. You should not feel pressure to get married and have a family at an age that you don't want that to happen, just because everyone else is doing it. There are no rules in this world about how to live your life. Be yourself and do what you love. Everything else will come right to its place, stop forcing things.

Staring at a computer screen or a TV will not bring you any clarity or wisdom. You need to stop wasting time watching reality shows or looking at Instagram pages and other social media. The harsh truth is that it is indeed brainwashing you and altering your mind, making you think incorrectly. Each time you open up Instagram and you take a look at how the celebrities and the rich people live, and you create false expectations in your mind about how you should live, and if you don't get that kind of life, you are disappointed by yourself and you think that you are miserable. You keep looking at models that wear expensive pieces of clothes that cost over ten thousand dollars and you think that you are poor and unhappy, when in fact you really aren't. Remember that there are people in this world without a roof over their heads and without clean water to drink that usually die from infections and other diseases, do you really think that they care about Instagram followers or expensive brands and designer clothes? I don't think so no. Most of the people are even addicted to such reality shows but they are not even aware of it. Kids nowadays tend to freak out if the internet connection or electricity goes out for a few minutes. It makes me feel like everyone is so addicted to living in the fake virtual social media worlds that it becomes utterly disgusting. I don't want to start that cliché talk about how we used to play hide and seek but kids nowadays don't because they are stuck in front of their computer screens, but when you really think about it, that "talk" slowly starts to become the sad reality. My honest opinion is that you should focus on doing things that will later help you ensure an existence for you, your family and your loved ones. If you really want to have a career in playing video games then yes, give your best and I hope you will make it, but if you spend your time on the internet watching celebrities and how they live while creating fake images of how you should live your life, then you are really harming yourself.

CHAPTER 4:

"Thinking outside of the box"

Most people don't think outside of the box, not because they can't but because they are afraid of being judged or being called "weird". Just like the example which I mentioned before about the guy who followed religion and religious traditions just because his family was doing it.

The truth is that we are all weird in a different way. Each of us is unique and we need to understand and embrace that. The sooner we realize this, the better for us.

Lateral thinking arises from the way our mind works. Our information handling system that is called "mind" is highly effective but it has its own limitations. Those

LATERAL THINKING

limitations are inseparable from the advantages of the system because both are coming directly from the nature of the system. It is impossible to get the advantages without the disadvantages. Lateral thinking is meant to compensate for the disadvantages while you can still enjoy the advantages.

Most people believe that the traditional so-called "vertical thinking" is the only possible and effective way of thinking. We need to look at the lateral thinking and understand how it works so that we can recognize the advantages compared to the vertical thinking method.

Vertical thinking is all about **rightness**, lateral thinking is all about **richness**. Vertical thinking often selects one path and excludes all of the other pathways. Lateral thinking works very differently. Instead of excluding paths it creates new paths that are otherwise invisible with vertical thinking.

With vertical thinking, a person will select the most promising approach when attempting to solve a problem. With lateral thinking, the person will try to generate as many different and alternative approaches possible. **If there's no way, you need to make one.** Vertical thinking takes you on a pathway only if one exists, lateral thinking helps you create a pathway. A lot of pathways.

With vertical thinking, a person will use the "negative" in a situation to be able to block and eliminate certain paths. With lateral thinking, there will be no "negative" in a situation. Lateral thinking is all about the "Glass half full, not half empty" approach.

One of the most perfect examples of lateral thinking and creating pathways or "Thinking outside the box" that I've ever heard is this one:

A guy is asked the following:

You are driving in your car on a very rainy day on your way home, and you get close to a bus stop. You slow down a bit and look at the people waiting in the rain with no ride. You look closely and realize that one of them is your best friend who once saved your life, the other one is the perfect woman of your dreams and the third one is a lonely old lady that looks really sick.

You can only take one person in your car and take them home. Which person would you choose? The people who asked him this thought that they tricked them because no matter what he chose he had to give up on something that is important to him. Do you pick up the old lady because she is in a very bad condition, or do you pick your best friend because he once saved your life? Either way, you are losing the woman of your dreams that you always loved.

The answer that he gave stunned everyone in the room. This is what he said:

I would give the keys of my car to my friend, he can drive the old lady back home and then get home safely himself, he will return the car later or tomorrow, and I will stay with the woman of my dreams and wait for the bus together.

This guy literally got the best possible outcome from the given situation. A prime example of lateral thinking and very good decision making abilities. He did not exclude all of his options in order to get only one and use that one. He instead made many new pathways and solved many problems at once, unlike the vertical thinking method which would've solved only one problem.

Now a vertical thinker would start excluding options, in this case, people, and find what option will benefit him the most. Then he would only take one person at home in his car and constantly try and convince himself that there was only one good choice and that he had gotten the most out of the situation. "I couldn't help everyone so I had to pick one". This is not right.

From our early kindergarten days to our late college graduation days we are being trained and taught to focus on getting good test grades and not on thinking outside the box and using our brain in a more creative way to solve problems easier. We only care about the outcome but not the process which is far more important. This is not good. This is just being trained to use vertical thinking. Instead, we should teach ourselves to use the lateral method.

You must always question yourself before making any decision. Why am I doing this? What is the best way to do it? What will the outcome of my decision be? Do I truly want this? Why do I want this? What are all the pathways that I can create? What are all the options that I can combine together in order to bring the best out of my current situation?

Understanding why you truly want something will make it easier for you to **create** the best way to do it and that will usually be something that is "outside of the box".

Some people just don't want to accept lateral thinking as a valid thinking method because it makes them feel like it threatens the validity of the more famous vertical thinking method. This is not the point of lateral thinking at all. Both of the processes are complementary, not antagonistic. Lateral thinking is very useful for generating ideas, creating different pathways and solutions or approaches, and vertical thinking is useful for developing them. Wise people would use lateral thinking to enhance and increase the effectiveness of their vertical thinking method by offering it more options to select from. Vertical thinking, on the other hand, will multiply the effectiveness of their lateral thinking method by making good a very good use of the ideas generated by it.

Most of the time a person might be using vertical thinking but when a situation calls for lateral thinking he needs to understand that no excellence in vertical thinking will solve the problem. To keep trying and persisting with vertical thinking in a situation that needs lateral thinking can be dangerous and lead to very bad decision making that might impact one's life. A wise person would be skilled in both thinking methods, and a master thinker would be able to combine them both in order to get the best out of the two worlds.

Here's a good example that might help you understand it visually. Imagine a car. That car has a reverse gear.

You simply cannot drive the car in reverse gear all the time because that's stupid.

On the other hand, you must have it and know how to use it because sometimes in your life you get stuck in a blind alley. Then you need to apply the reverse gear or in this case, the "Lateral thinking method" to get out of it.

Vertical and lateral thinking are not that much different. Both can be useful in a given situation. It's not about one way being so much more effective than the other. They are both necessary. It is a matter of being able to recognize the differences and advantages/disadvantages of both methods in order to be able to combine their use effectively.

CHAPTER 5:

Why we must think differently?

People are creatures of habit. Every single day they wake up on the same side of their beds and put on the same type of clothes they wore yesterday, they usually cook up the same breakfast and sit in the exact same car, take the same routine to their school or workplace and when they finally get there they do the same chores just like every other day, all over and over again.

Imagine being very old and almost finished with your life. All you have left is your memories and stories which left a mark in your mind. When that moment comes, do you really think that you will feel satisfied and fulfilled if you spent your entire life doing what others did and trying to impress the people around you? I think not. You will be full of regret, grief and constantly blame yourself for not living the way you truly wanted. So you should wake up before it is too late. You might feel comfortable now because you have no challenges, nothing to stand up for and everyone is normal towards you because you're doing everything exactly like them, but being in your comfort zone does not always mean being happy. In fact, it almost never means that you're happy.

We have only one life and our time is ticking away. Can you think of a person that wasn't different but left a mark in history? I know I can't. If you are just like everyone else and just another sheep in the herd nobody will ever talk about you and you won't be interesting to no one.

You need to ask yourself if you are truly happy with your current state and the current place that you are in. Are you getting the best out of your life? Are you truly living the way you want? Is there something that you're not doing just because you think that everyone else would laugh at you or think you're weird because of it?

Have you been taking any challenges lately? Are you "daring greatly"? Or are you just living like a timid soul who does not know about a victory or a defeat?

LATERAL THINKING

Something has to change if you are not happy. Life is a wonderful journey full of great and exciting stories and experiences. You can't let yourself live like a bird in a cage. Spread your wings and fly far away. Stop worrying about what others think. Leave the TV alone, you don't need it. Stop wasting time on social media, go out and meet new people. Expand your horizons. Listen to your heart.

Stop fearing failure. Many people want to do something, but they are just so afraid that they are going to fail at it that they don't even attempt doing it. One of the key problems here also comes from our childhood. The fear of failure almost always comes from an early age when we get destructive criticism from our parents for failing at something. Some people who suffer from this simply get paralyzed when they are offered an opportunity to do something different and exciting in their life. They will just give up on it before even trying and then spend many hours and sleepless nights convincing themselves that it was a good decision and they wouldn't have made it anyway even if they tried. It is hard to change something that has been carved into our heads from a very young age, but it is not impossible. We need to train our minds to look at the rewards and positive experiences that we will get out of the situation, even if we somehow manage to fail. Failures are nothing but lessons in life. And they are the most valuable ones. Nothing is a better teacher than a failure.

Take a look at this example of poor and wealthy people.

Rich people always try and manage to find a way to create more value, to produce and develop services and products that will enhance and enrich the lives and work of many people. Rich people almost always tend to put in tons of effort before they take out. They don't believe in something called "easy money" or getting something for free or nothing. They believe that you must work, earn and pay for what you're getting. On the other hand, poor people lack this type of understanding and they only see the option of putting as little effort as possible to get as much out of the situation as they can. They are always out trying to get something for free or for as little as possible. They all want success without effort, getting riches without labor, getting money out of the sky with no effort and achieving fame without possessing any talent. They gamble, buy tickets for the lottery, go to their workplaces in the last possible minute, waste their time while they are there trying to do anything else but working and then leave in the first minute possible.

LATERAL THINKING

They waste their money, time and energy on methods that are supposed to bring them wealth or fame without any effort, not realizing that all of that time can be used to improve themselves as people and increase their skill in doing something that is actually worth doing. Lining up by thousands of people for auditions such as American idol without even having elementary talent and skill to participate will bring you nothing but disappointment and wasted time.

One of the biggest secrets to becoming wealthy and successful is to always give your maximum no matter how much you are being paid. If you always tend to do this, the universe will simply find a way to put you in the place that you deserve, someone will recognize your skill and talent and take you to a better place where you can truly show up your work for what it's worth.

Always make sure to go the extra mile. Always tend to put in far more than you're willing to take.

In my experience, poor people tend to use the vertical thinking method only without combining it with all the pathways that lateral thinking can open up for them. They always tend to exclude one out of two options and go with the one that seems better for them at the moment instead of combining every other detail in order to get the best out of the situation that they're in.

And it not just about being wealthy or poor. Giving our best in every single situation of our lives will help us be the better person that we all want to be. It does not necessarily mean that it can only be applied in school or at your workplace. Any activity that you do always gives your best to do it with maximum effort. People will appreciate you a lot more.

CHAPTER 6:

Risk management, fear of making decisions and changes.

In this chapter, I will talk to you about Risk management and the fear that some people have when it comes to making a certain decision.

Some people are not fully using their thinking abilities and the entire capacity of their mind, simply because of the conditioning that they went through while they were growing up, which made them have this fear mentality. I will list some of the reasons why people are afraid to think differently.

For example, in the middle (dark) age, people that had different thoughts about religion or anything else were considered heretics or witches and they were burned alive, beaten or stoned to death. Even great minds such as Galileo Galilei were "bullied" in some way for thinking differently.

Thinking almost always brings somewhat of a change. And people are afraid of changes.

Thinking deeply about something can uncover some deeply buried memories, questions about life, make us reconsider our way of living or make us realize that we're doing something wrong but we're so deep into our comfort zones that we got used to it. Even though changes are a necessary part of our spiritual growth, some people are really afraid of them.

If you don't allow some space for changes in your life, you will stop growing spiritually. And if you stop growing spiritually you will be very unhappy with who you are and always feel like you're lost and alone. And although you maybe will feel safe and secure by never taking or accepting any challenges or risks, you will always be filled with regrets for not daring to grab some of the changes or opportunities that life gave you.

Thinking can bring us doubt and insecurity, as well as responsibility.

A lot of people simply choose to be ignorant, they are afraid that by thinking they will ruin their lives. For example, some people that are very religious just because someone else told them to be, are afraid of thinking about it because they might start questioning their beliefs and the entire religion. This might be a silly example but trust me, I know people who are afraid to question their religion and beliefs because they think when the time comes they will be sent to hell for doing it, so they just keep pretending that everything they heard or read about it is true without even trying to understand it. Ignorance is bliss.

Thinking can make us aware of some problems that are currently a part of our lives and urge us to find solutions for them. For some people, such realizations can be sometimes very painful and hard to swallow. This makes them not want to face their problems and just keep telling themselves that everything in their life is the way it should be.

Freedom and responsibility almost always go together in the same package. But, people hate taking responsibilities so they don't embrace freedom. Ever since our young age, we learn to place the responsibilities to someone else's shoulders, blame others for certain situations and for the kind of life they're living, without ever criticizing ourselves. We tend to always comment about others but never about us. We never look at ourselves and our own mistakes that we make in each day of our lives. The number of times we lied to someone we love or said something that hurt somebody else. Taking a look at ourselves means that we will find many flaws because nobody in this world is perfect, and this will always bring responsibilities which people tend to hate so much. And what is the best and easiest way of avoiding such responsibilities? Stop thinking and let others think for us. Don't stress yourself and let somebody else do all of the dirty work for you. Just sit back and criticize others and comment on their flaws. Sadly this is what the majority of people do. This is also the reason why we give the power to politicians and other sorts of leaders. We believe that they can fix all of our problems and that they are the "savior". Nobody can save us from our flaws and the insecurities that each one of us has. We cannot run from our problems and responsibilities forever. They will eventually catch us, trust me, they really will. The only way to deal with this is to face yourself and start making a change. No problem can be solved by running far away from it. It can only become bigger and harder to deal with when the time comes. And the time always comes.

We always think that if someone else changes the world will be a better place, but we never try to change ourselves because we are so afraid and insecure, our egos are high yet fragile. Change starts from within. **Change starts with who you are. Be the change you want to see in this world.**

You need to understand that changes cannot happen overnight. You cannot change who you are in just a couple of hours or even days or months. You need to start improving step by step, each day is a new opportunity to be a better person. **Changes are good, we need changes. Everything around us changes as each second passes by.**

Let's take a look at some of the changes that are fun to do and usually help us discover new things about ourselves but also help us deal with problems more easily.

Travel

A wise person once said: "The world is a book, and those who do not travel can only read one page of it."

I'm sure we've all heard stories or watched a movie about a famous businessman who after years of work decides to sell everything he owns and just travel the world as much as he can. To be honest, this is not very rare anymore. People get obsessed with traveling more and more because slowly everybody is realizing its benefits. It is one of the best changes that you can make in your life. You meet new people and create beautiful memories of many different and wonderful places. Traveling is also proven to be one of the best cures for depression, anxiety, and narrow-mindedness. When people finally return to their homes after a long journey, they are simply not the same anymore. They are a better version of themselves. Even short trips have the same benefits and they can also serve as a starting point for people who are just getting into traveling. Traveling makes you explore different cultures and lifestyles that can often help you overcome some insecurity that you have about yourself for being different than the others. For example, you can meet people that have the same interests as you and you will feel much warmer and like a good fit when you're among those people that you share common ground with. It also makes you feel much better outside of your comfort zone. People who do not travel have a very small comfort zone and even going to the closest grocery store can feel like something intimidating to them. This also indirectly impacts your confidence levels. People who travel more are more confident than people who don't. A truly undeniable fact is that facing new experiences helps people build confidence. Believe it or not, it can also impact your decision-making abilities and make you a better thinker. The ability to make certain decisions is important, yes, but imagine having to make decisions when you're alone in a foreign country. It is simply a very good practice that will help you become much better. Travelers also tend to utilize Lateral Thinking a lot. When you travel you only rely on yourself and the choices that you and only you make. This forces you to think outside of the box and make sure you get the best possible outcome out of every situation that you find yourself in during your journeys.

Traveling helps you learn your true self and find out things about you that you never really knew. This is one of the most important things and advantages that traveling can offer to a person. There is nothing better than fully knowing yourself.

Traveling alone gives you the opportunity to spend lots of time on your own, think about your past and future and it helps you clear your mind and gets a better angle of view for the current problems in your life that need solving. When you are really far away from your friends, family, and society that you see every single day, you can truly be honest with yourself. Sooner or later, we all have to find out who we really are and who we really want to be in life, and traveling will only enhance this experience for us.

Talk to people more and open up to others about your beliefs and opinions

For some people, it sometimes might be a bit harder to open up to a person and reveal their vulnerable and private things, but trust me, it helped me tremendously. I was a very anxious person myself and I kept things really private for a long time. When I first started openly talking to someone it was a random stranger in a bar and we both shared very powerful and valuable thoughts. I found out that he is exactly like me and that he just wanted someone to talk to. Many people are in this situation. Talking to anyone about your problems will really help you out. It can be a friend, a parent, a girlfriend or a complete stranger. After that I felt really good and like I had a huge rockfall out of my chest. The relief was incredible. This is when I finally realized that I should stop living in a cave and start communicating with others some more. You will be surprised how many people are also socially anxious and afraid to talk to someone not knowing that you both share similar if not exactly the same problems. Also, if you're a more confident person that is not really anxious about talking to others, one of the best things that you can do for someone if you see that they're going through a tough period is to simply ask them what's wrong and talk to them. It will mean a world of a difference to them and they will forever appreciate you. I cannot explain to you how many times I had a problem and I thought I was alone in it just so I go meet my friends and they tell me they have the exact same problem and suddenly everything is much easier. Sharing with others is really important, but also make sure to listen to other people's problems as well if they need someone to lean on.

Be humble. It's not possible for you to learn and see things differently when you think you know everything already

Humility will make you the greatest person ever.

In today's world, everyone is pre-occupied with external looks, bragging about personal achievements, Instagram followers and whatnot. Everyone just wants to be at the center of attention and their biggest goals are getting rich and famous. People love being around a person that radiates humility because they know whatever they say is fully heard, they are fully seen and accepted for who they are by that person. That person just makes everyone feel better, so others value his/her presence a lot and consider it as a gift. People like these also tend to see life as a school, they know that nobody of us is perfect and they are always improving themselves through accepting constructive criticism and advice from others. They are open to new ideas and utilize them in ways that help them improve in every field. They accept their mistakes and are not stubborn when it comes to admitting when they've done something wrong. This takes us right into our next chapter dedicated to making mistakes and how to live with them.

CHAPTER 7:

Understanding that you cannot always be right

To some, admitting their mistakes is not easy at all, but this is a very crucial step when it comes to becoming a better person and an overall better thinker.

Learn from your mistakes and the mistakes of others. Study about other people's situations where they made a mistake and when it really made an impact on their lives. Think about different scenarios that you might find yourself in one day.

Remember, you can only learn from a mistake after you admit that you made it. If you're the type of person who instantly starts blaming others or even the entire universe for your own mistakes, you will never be able to utilize them as lessons in life. But, if you are bravely stand up and admit to yourself "This is my own mistake and my own responsibility" the chances of learning something and becoming a better person will be drastically increased. Since early school days, we're taught to feel guilty about failure and to do literally anything we can to avoid mistakes. Some kids are even taught to cheat on tests or exams just so that they won't get a bad grade and ruin their parent's reputation. This creates very bad habits and will later translate into a very bad person and low quality as a person. The sense of shame, fear of mistakes and yet another failure is what keeps many people away from goals and success.

Don't just admit in front of other people for the sake of admitting or so that you won't be considered ignorant. Truly admit it to yourself that you made it, and accept it. Every time you admit that you did a mistake you become a better person and you grow even more spiritually. Understand that you are not in control of this universe and that you don't know everything that's going on. Sometimes you are simply not right in an argument. Admit it. Don't force your own opinion on others.

Be wise. Don't just try to run away from the possible blame you might be getting. Don't try to blame someone else. Everybody makes mistakes. Admit.

Here's what it takes to be able to learn from your own mistakes:

Having some self-confidence to admit that you've made a mistake.

People who admit when they make a mistake are usually almost instantly forgiven and people have respect for them. The ones who never admit and keep running from them or blame others are usually the ones that nobody enjoys being around.

Being brave and courageous when it comes to making a change.

For example, if a friend tells you that you are always being stubborn in an argument, even when you are not necessarily right, instead of starting another pointless argument with him as well, you need to take this advice and really think about it. If you really know that this is true, you need to be brave and consider making a change. I know a lot of people that simply always want to be right, even when they are not. People don't enjoy being around an ignorant and stubborn person. Don't be that guy.

Practicing by creating different scenarios and situations with many possible outcomes in your mind

This is a method that I use and it really helped me a lot.

Create interesting situations and scenarios in your head where you can make a mistake or where you've already made one, and work from there. Try to fully visualize and understand the situation and using the lateral thinking method that I talked about earlier, try to combine all of the pathways in order to create the best possible outcome from the situation. Practice this often and you will soon find out that you are able to deal with situations much easier, and instead of blaming others for your mistakes, you will simply not make them anymore.

CHAPTER 8:

Your emotion is your only compass. Learn to always listen to your heart.

I know that each one of us has an Inner Compass built inside that provides us with guidance about what is the best way forward for us. But the question that everyone wants to know the answer to is how does it actually do this? How does it guide us? The simple answer is that it goes through our emotions. They are the most powerful thing that we possess. Let's take a closer look at this.

Everyone knows when something feels good or bad, everyone knows the difference between feeling angry and feeling love, between feeling depressed and feeling joyful… but what most of us don't understand or realize is that these emotions are important indicators because they are giving us vital information about what is going on in our lives.

When you stop and notice what's going on inside you, you will see you are probably experiencing a wide range of emotions, emotions which vary depending on the situation you are in. Whether it's what's going on in your family or what's happening as you interact with your partner or your colleagues at work. But it does not matter if we are aware of this mechanism or not, our emotions are still there and they exist. All of the time. This means that even if we like it or not, every single one of us has an inner compass that will keep providing us with this information through our emotions.

Live in harmony, fully understand, accept and embrace who you are.

So when you and what you are thinking and doing are in alignment with who you really are and what's best for you, you are in harmony with who you really are. This translates into a feeling of joy, flow, ease, and happiness because you are living in alignment with your true nature, your deeper essence, or you could say with your soul essence. And then, the connection is open between you and the Great Universal Intelligence that is orchestrating the dance of Life. So Life feels good and is good and you are in flow – and things just seem to work out better for you.

When you're doing something that you don't really enjoy doing, you know it. Your mind and body will simply give you a signal that what you're doing is just not right for you. For example, if you prefer hanging out in the park with a more "alternative" type of people instead of going to the mainstream clubs and discos, spend your time where you prefer spending it more. It is your own life with your own rules and nobody can tell you what to do or where you should go. If some of your friends prefer going out and partying every day but you want to read a book instead, you should not force yourself to go with them. Yes, you might want to try it once or twice to see if you really like it, but if you find yourself sitting awkwardly in the middle of the club not talking to anyone and on top of that you hate the type of music playing in the background, why would you keep doing it? I agree that there are some things in life that we simply don't know if we like until we try them, but if you see that it is just not right for you after a couple attempts... Don't force anything. **Apply lateral thinking in these kinds of situations**

Listening to your heart

Learn to listen to your feelings and emotions. I think that each one of us is born with an ability to sense when something is "right" or "wrong" for us. We should not mistake this with letting only our emotions or animalistic behavior take over. Everything in moderation. We must not suppress our logic and reasoning. But, sometimes the heart is the one with the smarter decision. Since the beginning of our adolescence period, we are somehow "trained" of always finalizing a decision by using rationality and logic that our brain provides. Especially when we need to make a life-changing decision. But, not every decision brought by our brain is necessarily right. Logic and reason can sometimes fool us into believing that what we decided is best for us, which leaves our heart outvoted and left behind. Try to imagine the severe consequences when a person is supposed to

LATERAL THINKING

change his workplace in order to get a bigger salary but the job requires him to go far away from home. Yes, the brain will make you bring a decision based on the current financial state but the heart knows that you simply don't want to leave your home and family and go work overboard. The heart does not care about getting more money or luxury, but it does care about your home, family and their good being and happiness.

The mind is capable of creating the most beautiful works of art, it serves as the source of scientific brilliance and an origin of inventive solutions to many complicated problems. But, it is also often caught up in the boundaries of physical life and the drama and fear that surround us daily. When you're facing a problem, the mind will come up with a reasonable conclusion and this is why we're tempted to accept that one as the right one, but there is nothing more powerful than feeling a strong signal from your heart when it comes to making a certain decision, and we've all felt this before. Love, for example, is the strongest emotion that a human being can feel. And not just humans, animals feel love too. If you were in love before you know how it feels and how nothing can even compare to it. In fact, this emotion is so strong that even science cannot explain how in certain moments it can suppress all other also strong emotions like fear and such. For example when a mother lifted an entire car to save her baby that was trapped under it, or when a dog that loves his owner will fight against ten other dogs just to save him even when it clearly knows that he will lose the battle and most likely end up dying or getting injured really badly. This only shows us why love is the most powerful emotion, and we all know that it comes from the heart. So listen to your heart when it signals you.

Conclusion

Every morning when we wake up, we have a decision to make. Starting from a very simple one like: "Which shirt should I wear today?" or "Should I eat lunch now or after work?" to some more complex ones like accepting a different job that is abroad and such. But, the most important decision that we are supposed to make do we want to be a better version of ourselves today or not. Each day we are given a chance to make a significantly important change in this world. The only question is are we willing to take it. Every one of us lives a different life, filled with countless different stories and experiences, but we are all humans and we live on the same planet. We need to stop looking at races, colors, religions and anything else that is used to separate us from one another. We all face the same problems and each day we give our best to think our way out of them. We think just as much as we breathe, which obviously means that we should give as much effort to thinking as we do to breathing. I want everyone who is reading this book to understand that we are unique and we possess different qualities that we can use to make this world a better place.

We can help each other and we can use our minds in a much more positive way, not for destruction, creating wars and bringing tears to others. We are created and brought on this Earth to be much more than that. We have been given a magnificent brain capable of solving the most complex problems that we can imagine. Stop wasting time on social media, stop being worried about how you look and stop buying expensive clothes, you don't need them to look good. Positive energy is the only thing you need to attract others. Stop looking at that Instagram follower count, appreciate people for who they are, not for the number of likes they have on Facebook. Find someone to love, leave your comfort zone and enjoy life.

There is so much to explore and so many people to meet out there. Staring at your computer screen or

LATERAL THINKING

your TV will never bring you any good memories or unforgettable experiences. Stop allowing the news or other propaganda to brainwash you and alter the way you think. Don't be a part of the herd. Don't be a sheep. Everything that happens in life happens for a reason. And everything that happens can be either a good or a bad thing. And this depends on you. Only on you. Every situation can be considered a lesson. Every experience should be a gift. Look on the bright side of life. A positive attitude and strong spiritual mindset will make you far greater than you are and take you a long way. Believe in your dreams. Success can be achieved as long as you keep believing. You can do everything you want if you set your mind on it. Be brave, be strong, be smart and care for others. Radiate positive energy and good vibes, people will love being around you.

Be a good thinker, make great decisions and arguments but don't insist that you are always right in every situation. Learn from others, if someone has something to say let them say it, they may be share tons of knowledge that they would like to share. You never know how wise someone really is if you don't let them talk. Find balance in everything. It's the key to living a good and happy life. You are the creator of your own destiny. Just like you should balance both thinking methods that I talked about in this book. Leave your insecurities behind, don't try to seek perfection in everything. Everyone has flaws. Don't be ashamed of them. Instead, try and work on them so that they become advantages instead of flaws. Turn the situation and current state into your own favor. Be yourself and people will enjoy being around you. I believe that there is a perfect match for everyone on this Earth, you just have to go out and meet them. And that does not happen in a comfort zone. Whenever you feel like you're alone in something, remember that there are countless other people who feel exactly the same. If you need help ask for it. If you feel depressed or anxious just talk to someone. It will make you feel so much better. Humans are created to help each other. We all radiate energy that can be used for a good cause.

Stay safe and remember: Your mind is the ultimate creation capable of solving every puzzle, there is always a solution to the problem that you have, and the only thing that you need to do, is just keep searching until you find the missing piece.

I hope that this book helped everyone who read it. I hope that you understood and learned something from my previous experiences, situations, and examples. Remember to always stay strong and remain on your own path. We only have one life and time is ticking away, so use it wisely. A Kung-Fu master once said:

*"You are too concerned with what was and what will be. Yesterday is history, tomorrow is a mystery, but today is a gift. That is why it is called **the present**."*

BONUS CHAPTERS:

From " The Power of Opportunity"

by Chris Smythe

In a world flooded with competition, be it in finding the right life partner, the right job or learning to have a sound connection with your family and finances, one can be stripped off opportunities. Yes, there are plenty of opportunities to go around but what if you are the unlucky one who is not getting them? Why should you sit there and sulk? Why should you be waiting for an opportunity to find you, when you can get up and actually create your own?

LATERAL THINKING

Gone are the days when you could depend on your luck and wait for opportunities to knock at your door. Life moves at a fast pace and sometimes there is no looking back to decisions taken in life. Wise people know and understand the importance of creating opportunities and through this book "The Power of Opportunity"; you will be provided with the knowledge that can help you master the art of creating opportunities. When you learn and make yourself capable of attracting the right people and energy, you open magical doors of opportunities for you and for others around you.

There are countless people out there, uninformed and unaware of the wonderful opportunities surrounding them every single day. Instead of recognizing and utilizing these opportunities, they end up heading in the wrong direction. This is due to the lack of awareness that they have and wrong attitude towards thinking that they cannot get anything better. When you do not make use of opportunities and cannot create them for yourself, you waste your time and energy with people, jobs and decisions that will do you no good in life.

So why should you be amongst the unlucky ones when you have the perfect chance to change your life? Why should you be the unhappy employee stuck with the same job for life? It is never too late to learn the importance of creating opportunities. Presented in this book are the best methods through which you can be an opportunity magnet. If you follow the guidelines and understand the essence of keeping the right mental attitude, you will soon find yourself with wondrous opportunities that you never even imagined having.

Your Attitude Determines How Successful You Can Be

Not every day is the same; every moment brings with it a fair share of happiness, joy, grief, and sadness. Unfortunate as it may be, that is the number one rule of life. Waiting for happiness to knock at your door, or waiting for the tides of grief to subside, is not how it works. Struggle is the keyword here if you want to achieve anything in life, or simply move on from a current state of mind, you need to buck up, hold your head up high and "strive" through thick and thin in life.

In order to reach anywhere in life, you need to develop the right attitude. You ask what is the right attitude? The right kind of attitude cannot be objectively determined; it can have various interpretations, depending on the situation at hand. It may simply mean going for a jog to clear your head or standing up for what you believe in, even when the winds are in the opposite direction.

If you want to weather any kind of storm in your life, you need to have the right attitude. The right attitude not only helps you focus and get out of a certain situation or predicament, but it also helps you identify opportunities, which might open up doors to self-improvement and enhancement if nothing else.

As they say, an opportunity never knocks twice; try to make the most of your present; soak in each moment as it is and grab each opportunity that comes by. Live in the present; learn from your past and start preparing for your future, but also know that nothing in this world will last forever. Having said this, living in the moment does not imply that you become ignorant about your future. The right approach towards life, in general, is to be as proactive as possible and to foresee any changes or evolutions in the future.

Evolve as a Human Being

Develop the Right Attitude

Having elaborated upon the importance of developing the right attitude, it is crucial to identify the nature of the attitude. According to various optimists, adopting a positive outlook towards life is the right way to perceive life. If you are wondering how to inculcate positivity in your life, give the below a good read:

Happiness is a Choice

Engulfed in an ocean of troubles, sorrows, and grief makes it increasingly hard for you to re-surface and acknowledge the existence of a lifeboat or an island, by the corner. This simply means that whenever you are depressed or troubled, you tend to ignore that tiny flicker of hope and fail to consider happiness as an option for you. This is where having a positive attitude would help you and make you realize that happiness is just around the corner. But only if you are ready to embrace it.

You need to find the good in the ugly, a light in the darkness and a rose in a bush of thorns. The process of treating happiness as a choice and then pursuing it is no piece of cake. It requires a tremendous amount of perseverance, self-resolve and most of all, the willingness to dust yourself up. However, you need to realize that happiness hardly ever comes as an uninvited guest. Just like everything else in life, you need to strive for happiness and, many times, this struggle might turn out to be the most difficult of all.

Learn to Prioritize

Prioritizing your life, in terms of the most and least important tasks, not only gives you perspective, it encourages you to think positively. The outcome of prioritizing is always beneficial for you and the people around you. Thus, prioritize your life in the following way:

Reinstate Your Purpose

Time and again, you need to keep reminding yourself of your purpose in life. Years of pain and suffering might have blurred your sense of purpose, but you need to try to rekindle that flame. Try to redirect your life to a time when you truly felt happy and then reassess. Try to question yourself, what changed and why? Try to assess your situation and try to carve a way forward.

Identify Your Purpose

Having reflected upon your actions and words should give you sufficient food for thought to identify your sense of purpose. Start by prioritizing your responsibilities and see where your loyalties should lie, at work or at home. Chalk out a list of positive attributes you wish to develop with time and think of various ways to accomplish them.

Visualize Your Future

Form a clear picture of where you want to see yourself in the next 2 to 3 years. Hang on to that visual picture; if nothing else, it would motivate you to become what you aspire to be.

Look For Positivity Around You

Believe it or not, there is a speck of positivity even in the most negative and darkest of all situations. You might not be able to discover it with the naked eye; you need to use your inner eye to see beyond all the negativity. Faith and belief should be the two constants in your life and they will help you see the light at the end of the tunnel. Whatever happens in your life is a learning experience and take upon every hardship as a challenge, only to resurface as a survivor, stronger and more powerful than ever before.

Listen to Your Inner Voice

No matter how many motivational sessions you attend, unless you listen to your inner voice and talk to it, you will never develop the will to power through.

Having said this, do not let your inner voice dominate you and try to reason with it.

Remove Negativity From Your Life

If you are trying to be positive, you cannot afford to surround yourself with negative people. They will simply discourage you and dampen your spirits. Moreover, try to rid yourself of negative thoughts, actions, and things. The aim is to build a positive aura around yourself and not to let any unnecessary negativity seep through.

Looking at the Bright side

What is the bright side? Have you ever really given it a thought? Some people simply cannot acknowledge the greener side of the pasture, especially when they are buried under the rubble of troubles and sorrows. What they fail to understand is that the hope of a brighter side is going to help them survive and wage all of life's battles. Even when you see no light at the end of the tunnel, you need to believe that it exists and the only way you can get there is by being optimistic.

For those who have given up hope and are finding it extremely hard to get out of their current predicament, looking at the bright side is not at all easy. For such people, the following tips might come in handy:

Accept Life

The fundamental step towards a happy and contented life is to embrace life with open arms. Instead of whining over petty issues and your current state of affairs, learn to accept each facet of life, no matter how ugly or unpleasant it may be. Things just do not happen, the sooner you realize this, the better it will be for you. If you want to change your life, you need to take control and take the necessary steps to right all the wrongs. Always remember that time and tide waits for no one; your fate is in your hands.

Remind Yourself that You are Capable

At times, we don't know just how strong we are, unless being strong is the only option we are left with. You need to remind yourself, over and over again, that you are capable of dealing with whatever comes your way. Do not let your caste, profession or your relationships define who you are. Your inner potential is hidden and only you can truly exploit it, especially during times when you are tested. Ignore the voices around you and assess yourself, then only can you truly determine the power and strength you have within.

Disregard Others' Opinions

We spend too much time fussing over what others think about us. This only makes us weak and dependent on people and soon enough, we start looking at the world from other people's eyes. Always remember, you are who you want to be and you can never become a figment of someone else's opinions unless you let them control your feelings and emotions. Analyze your inner strengths, weaknesses, and disregard what other people think of you. At the end of the day, you are your best judge and the way you know yourself, no one else does.

Stop Comparing Yourself to Others

The brighter side of life will cease to exist for you if you keep comparing yourself to others and complain about the blessings they have and you have been deprived of. If you have a habit of comparing, do it with someone who is less fortunate, so that you can count your bounties and become grateful. As for the voids you feel in your life, roll up your sleeves and strive to fill the gaps. What you need to believe is that your struggles, your faith, and your capabilities are more than enough for you to strive through your life.

Love Yourself

At times, when your faith is shaken, you tend to bury yourself under a pile of complexes and try to hide from the world. You need to realize that you need to start loving yourself before you can love others, be it people, your work or your external environment. Accept your weaknesses, bask in your qualities and try to love yourself, just the way you are. You need a reality check, every now and then, that whatever you are and whatever you have is enough to struggle through rough patches.

Keep Your Calm

Do not let others influence your behavior and no matter what they say or do, try to keep your calm, at all times. You do not want to find yourself in a situation where you end up acting irrationally, due to a nasty or ugly remark from a friend or family member. Always remember, you have everything at stake, you have everything to lose, not the other person. Therefore, be mindful of your behavior because, at the end of the day, you are the only one responsible for it.

Treat Life as a Journey

Do not yearn for the perfect destination in your life. Your entire life is a journey and it needs to be undertaken, one step at a time. Accept whatever life offers you and make the most of this journey, even if things do not work out the way you want them to. They never do, do they? Try to live in the moment, knowing that nothing lasts forever. This will make you appreciate the little things in life and give you the strength to tackle obstacles along the way.

Share Happiness

Share happiness and it will multiply. Ever heard this phrase? It is not only restricted to books of philosophy; it has a deeper meaning in life. Try to develop a positive outlook towards life and share that positivity with people around you. The aim is to share happiness and inculcate a feeling of mutual sharing and appreciation between your friends, family, and colleagues.

Keep the aforementioned tips in mind and try to implement them in your life, regardless of whether you are weathering a storm or contented with your life. Positivity doesn't develop overnight; it takes considerable time and patience to look at the brighter side and to maintain that outlook, even during hardships and difficulties.

Always remember that life does not stay the same, all the time. Change is the only constant in life and the sooner you learn to be positive, the easier it would be for you to embrace the bitter reality of life. A little patience, perseverance, and faith would go a long way. Rest assured, being an optimist would surely pay off, if not now, then in the long run.

Step Out of Your Comfort Zone

In order to achieve anything worthwhile in life, you need to make an effort; there is nothing like a "free lunch" in life. Yes, good things come to those who wait, but opportunities do not knock on those doors, where people are too comfortable with their current way of living.

The first and foremost rule of accomplishment is to step out of your comfort zone, do things which you never thought you were capable of, say things which were never said before and tackle obstacles along the way. You cannot expect your fate to do marvels for you, without even twitching a single muscle and making the tiniest bit of effort. If you are truly determined to achieve something, make that your aim or goal and give it all you have got.

If nothing else, stepping out of your comfort zone would expose you to a different facet of life and will enrich you with such a learning experience, the likes of which cannot be found in textbooks or motivational lectures. Life is surely a gamble, you need to play your cards wisely and always remember that risk and certainty are part and parcel of the game.

If you are wondering how to step out of the safety shell that you have built around yourself, here are a few helpful tips:

Embark on a Different Journey

If you truly want to step out of your comfort zone, try doing something different and ambitious. Until now, you might be used to doing activities and tasks, which were aligned with your personality. This puts a cap on the nature and type of experiences that you are exposed to. Try to do something which contradicts your personality and is a little demanding, so that you can experience something new and exciting. You never know, you might end up surprising yourself or the people around you.

Embrace Your Fears

The fear of a bad outcome or the fear of failure usually stops people from stepping out of their comfort zones and striving to accomplish something meaningful in life. If you want to approach a certain loved one and express your feelings, the fear of rejection and being let down might stop you from entering the battlefield, with your head held up high. You need to face your deepest and darkest fears and embrace them, as a part of life. Failure to do so would impair your ability to bring about significant changes in your life.

Many people have such strong fears that it becomes next to impossible for them to overcome them. Having said that, this process cannot be completed overnight, it takes a lot of time and dedication. The trick is to take one step at a time and let yourself get used to the fractional changes, instead of drastic ones.

Involve People

Before embarking upon a new journey, involve a friend or loved one. You would be surprised to find out how much that would help. Having someone by your side, one who is facing the exact same things that you are, is soothing and comforting, at the end of the day. However, if your journey is all about self-exploration and self-assessment, involving a third person would fail to do the trick. Several journeys are meant to be embarked alone so that you can truly capture the essence of the experiences you face along the way.

Make New Friends

Many times, when you are desperate to step out of your comfort zone, the best way is to stop hanging out with your current group of friends. Try befriending someone, with diverse interests and hobbies and you will see a noticeable change in your thoughts and actions. A person's company plays a vital role in his/her personality development and what better way to change your perspective towards life than to make a new friend.

Think of Positive Memories

Stepping out of your comfort zone usually means focusing on the positives and ignoring the negative voices inside your head. Before delving into something completely new and different, think of the last time you stepped out of your comfort zone and try to relive the positive memories of that specific incident. Negative thoughts would automatically perturb you and would distract you from your main goal and/or purpose. Do not let them get in the way of trying out something different. Adopting a tunnel vision approach would probably work best here. Therefore, eyes should be on the prize and the only way you can get hold of the prize is by thinking positive.

Do Your Homework

Sometimes your imagination becomes your worst enemy and tries to paint a gruesome picture of whatever you are delving into. Being double-minded is completely natural, but you need to exercise a bit of self-control over your thoughts. Try to do a bit of research on whatever it is that you want to try and experiment. Try to track down various other people who have embarked upon the same path and gauge their experiences, thoughts, and reactions. Rest assured, a positive word of mouth would benefit you greatly.

Other Techniques

Stepping out of your bed of roses always requires a high level of control of the mind, over your body. In order to reach such a level of control, you need to soothe your emotional state of mind. You need to have faith; you need to believe in yourself and your inner capabilities. The following might help you stabilize your emotional state of being:

- Use your imagination to your own advantage and try to let it wander in a positive manner. Try to form a rosy picture of how exciting and thrilling it would be to try something new and different.

- Food for thought is as important as food for the soul. Music is the most effective way to lift your spirits and helps you gain perspective.

- Practice a few breathing exercises on a daily basis, you would be surprised to find out just how effective they are.

- It's also helpful to take meditation classes and learn the various arts of meditation, yoga being the most popular one.

Five Ways to Be More Proactive

Do you know what it's like to be proactive? Have you ever given this nine-letter word some thought? There is a popular misconception that being proactive is strictly restricted to taking an initiative and making an effort. However, a proactive person plans each action, every step of the way and takes full accountability and responsibility for the decisions he/she makes along the way.

It is a shining attribute of a proactive person, not to play the blame game and to handle all the successes and failures that come along. A proactive person knows that failure is not an end, it is a means to an end and it only helps you realize your mistakes and prevents you from repeating them in the future. Being proactive gives you a renewed sense of purpose and teaches you not to blame anyone else for your actions and decisions. Life in general and the various challenges along the way become easier and manageable once you become proactive. If you want to become a proactive person, it is never too late to learn; follow the five essential ways listed below.

Prioritize Your Life

The most important step towards being proactive is to prioritize your life, each and every step of the way. You need to list down your roles and responsibilities, in order and evaluate the relative significance of each in your life. Try to strike a work/life balance and take into account your most valued relationships. Prioritizing your everyday tasks and relationships would, in other words, help you allocate your time and attention, ranging from the most to the least important task on your to-do list.

However, priorities tend to change over time and you need to accommodate them in your everyday life. For many people, their family is the topmost priority and for good reason. However, as your life changes, your priorities tend to change and you need to be flexible enough to make room for new people or responsibilities in your life's equation. It is advisable to schedule your life around your priorities, in order to do justice to yourself, your work and the people related to you.

Make Your To-Do List

Make it a habit, before sleeping every night, to draft your to-do list. If nothing, it will certainly give you a sense of purpose and direction. Chalk out all the activities, be if personal or work-related and write down their respective deadlines. Closely twined with the above point, making a to-do list makes you prioritize your life in a better and more efficient manner. A to-do list is practically a graphical representation of your mind map and lays down what needs to be done and when.

From a psychological perspective, it helps you plan for the near future, in a more constructive manner and helps you predict black swans along the way. What are black swans? They are giant, winged creatures, but not according to the current context. In truly marketing terms, black swans are referred to as events that cannot be predicted in the future and are outliers to the individual or business. The only way one can truly avoid them is by being proactive and planning out every single detail of his/her life.

State Your Outcomes

Failing to plan is planning to fail, right? This might sound like a cliché but has a profound meaning, especially when it comes to being proactive. An inherent part of planning is the process of objective and goal setting. After prioritizing your life and making a to-do list, you need to be clear about your goals and ambitions.

Ask yourself, what is it that you are trying to accomplish? How would you want to see yourself, say at the end of this week or month? Even if your priority is to join the gym and lose a few pounds, your outcome at the start and end of the time period should be clear and well defined. Try linking your objectives to your priorities and accomplish each, in the order of their relative importance. Paint a mental picture and try to use your imagination, in order to successfully define and implement your goals.

Determine High Payoff Activities

Setting your outcomes is always the toughest task and once you have established clear-cut objectives according to your priorities, you are now ready to start with the screening process. Assess each activity on your to-do list and question its importance and role in achieving the respective outcome. Tasks with greater importance and relevance should be included, whereas redundant ones should be crossed off your list.

After identifying your high payoff activities, you should focus on allotting a specific date and time to them, so that you do not end up doing something else in that time slot. Again, your high payoffs are dependent upon your priorities; the greater priority a task has, the higher would be the payoff.

Share Your Plans

The last step in being proactive is to share your plans with people- not everyone, only the ones you truly trust. It can be your spouse, your manager or even your boss. This is the time to reflect upon whatever you have worked for in the past week or month. Give them the accountability to question you on your daily or weekly progress, so that you can reflect on your actions and gauge the relative success or failure of your proactive behavior. Try to identify points of weaknesses and loopholes in the plans and take the necessary steps to rectify them in the future.

After discussing the five most crucial steps towards becoming a proactive individual, the relative importance of adopting this concept in your life should become clear. A proactive person is better able to deal with various unforeseen events, as opposed to a reactive person. A reactive person hardly plans and waits for the calamity to strike, before actually taking steps to rectify it. The choice is yours, at the end of the day: if you want to be prepared for the future, even to the slightest degree, being proactive is the way to be.

Thank you for reading "Lateral Thinking". If you enjoyed this book, please take the time to share your thoughts and consider leaving a review. Even if it's only a line or two; it would make all the difference and would be greatly appreciated.

Thank you *Chris Smythe*

www.ingramcontent.com/pod-product-compliance
Lightning Source LLC
Chambersburg PA
CBHW060408080526
44583CB00012B/506